ALSO BY ROCHELLE OWENS

Poetry

Not Be Essence That Cannot Be
Salt & Core
I am the Babe of Joseph Stalin's Daughter

Plays

Futz
The String Game
Homo
Istanboul
Beclch
He Wants Shih!
The Karl Marx Play
A Ritual
Baal Shem
Coconut Folk-Singer
Kontraption
Spontaneous Combustion Plays (editor)

THE JOE 82 CREATION POEMS

ROCHELLE OWENS

Los Angeles
BLACK SPARROW PRESS
1974

THE JOE 82 CREATION POEMS. Copyright © 1974 by Rochelle Owens. All rights reserved. Printed in the United States of America. No part of this book may be used or reproduced in any manner whatsoever without written permission except in the case of brief quotations embodied in critical articles and reviews. For information address Black Sparrow Press, P.O. Box 25603, Los Angeles, CA, 90025.

LIBRARY OF CONGRESS CATALOGING IN PUBLICATION DATA

Owens, Rochelle.
  The Joe 82 creation poems.

  I. Title.
PS3565.W57J6   811'.5'4   74-20591
ISBN 0-87685-217-7
ISBN 0-87685-216-9 pbk.

ACKNOWLEDGEMENTS: The author wishes to extend thanks to the editors of the following magazines where some of these works have appeared: *The American Poetry Review, Broadway Boogie, Burning Deck, Exile, New York Quarterly, The Paris Review, Partisan Review, Sun, Unmuzzled Ox.*

To the memory of my father
Max Bass

TABLE OF CONTENTS

Part 1: Magnetic Flux

- (I) The First Footsong Of Wild-Man 15
- (II) The Virgin's Baby Howling Boy Is Wild-Man's Christmas Song. 16
- (III) Wild-Man Eats Christmas Cake 17
- (IV) Wild-Man And The Woman Of The Stony Cave 18
- (V) Wild-Man On A Monday Nite 19
- (VI) Wild-Man Sees The Vinegar Rainbow 20
- (VII) Wild-Man Counts His Perfections 21
- (VIII) Wild-Man's Day B'fore New Year's Eve 22
- (IX) Wild-Man's Busted Beer Bottle 23
- (X) Wild-Man's Common Truth On New Year's . . . 24
- (XI) Wild-Man's View-Eye Of The Blessed 25
- (XII) The Birth Of Wild-Woman And/Or The Change 26
- (XIII) Wild-Woman Sharply And Triumphantly Watches 27
- (XIV) Wild-Woman & The Vegetation 29
- (XV) Wild-Woman & The Daemon In The Water . . . 30
- (XVI) Wild-Woman Sitting In The Center Of Water . . . 31
- (XVII) The Judgement In The Water And Song . . . 32
- (XVIII) Wild-Woman & The River & Moon 33
- (XIX) Wild-Woman Beholds The Sea's History . . . 34
- (XX) Wild-Woman In The Sea In The Long Day . . . 36
- (XXI) The Judgement Of Water 37
- (XXII) Wild-Woman And The Truth In The Water . . . 38

Part 2: The Enfolding

- (XXIII) Wild-Man In The Fascinating Forest 41
- (XXIV) Wild-Man In The Gethsemane Of The Forest . . 42
- (XXV) Wild-Man & The Temptation In The Forest . . . 44
- (XXVI) Wild-Man In The Essence Of The Forest 46
- (XXVII) Wild-Man In The Terror Of The Forest 48
- (XXVIII) Wild-Man In The Reversal Of The Terror 50
- (XXIX) Wild-Man & The Dream On The Forest-Edge . . 51
- (XXX) Wild-Man Speaks From The Nest Of Birds . . . 53
- (XXXI) Wild-Man Talking On The Nature Of His Form . . 54
- (XXXII) Wild-Man Names A Creature & Calls Water-Bright!. 55
- (XXXIII) Wild-Man & The Influence Of The She 56
- (XXXIV) Wild-Woman & The Invention Of Life 57
- (XXXV) Wild-Woman & The Song From The Breast . . . 58

(XXXVI)	Wild-Woman And The Wonder Of Fat, Honor and Death	59
(XXXVII)	Wild-Woman & The Joy Incantation Song	60
(XXXVIII)	Wild-Woman & The Shine Of Thought & Talk	62
(XXXIX)	Wild-Woman & The Leaping Ape	64
(XL)	Wild-Woman In The Middle Of The Hanging Tongues	65
(XLI)	Wild-Woman & The Taste Of The Wisdoms	67
(XLII)	Wild-Woman & The Premonition Of Technology	68
(XLIII)	Wild-Woman & The Second Moment Of Science	70
(XLIV)	Wild-Woman & The Naming Of Metal	72

Part 3: Fire Clay

(XLV)	Wild-Man & The Peeking Into The Cloud	75
(XLVI)	Wild-Man & The Righteous Perspective	76
(XLVII)	The Funnel Of Steel In The Green Forest Bush	77
(XLVIII)	Wild-Man & The Rhythm Of The Mechanized System	79
(XLIX)	Wild-Man & The Overhearing Of Disasters	81
(L)	Wild-Man & The Bad News Telegram	83
(LI)	Wild-Man & The Memory Of The Dying Poet	85
(LII)	Wild-Man & The Contemplation Of Lunar Incest	87
(LIII)	Wild-Man & The Essence Of The Crystal X-Rays	88
(LIV)	Wild-Man & The Reverberation Of Poetry	90
(LV)	The Organization In The Jungle	92
(LVI)	The Mystery Of Wild-Woman & The Perfect Peace	94
(LVII)	Wild-Woman & The Nature Of Horror & Love	96
(LVIII)	Wild-Woman & The Thinking-On Of Putrefaction	98
(LIX)	Wild-Woman And The Heart Of Things	100
(LX)	Wild-Woman And The Device Of Mangling	102
(LXI)	Wild-Woman And The Vale Of Bones	103
(LXII)	Wild-Woman & The Profound Wishing	104
(LXIII)	Wild-Woman In The Windless Night	105
(LXIV)	Breathing With Honey	106
(LXV)	The Victim Sings Freshly	108
(LXVI)	Wild-Woman & The Closeness Of The Gasp	109

Part 4: Basic Information

(LXVII)	The Equinox Commandment.	113
(LXVIII)	Kaddish For The Father	114
(LXIX)	The Wandering / The Poem For The Father	115
(LXX)	The Father Song—A Continuation	117
(LXXI)	The Father Weeping—& The Machine	118
(LXXII)	The Father Joy—The Running	120
(LXXIII)	The Young Father—But That Was In Another Country	122
(LXXIV)	The Spoken Father Word	124
(LXXV)	The Father Whispering Away In The Earth	125
(LXXVI)	The Father Whispering All The While	127
(LXXVII)	The Father Destiny—Love	129
(LXXVIII)	The Father Wounding Into Star	130
(LXXIX)	The Father's Looking-On & Proof	131
(LXXX)	Father's Expression Into Air	132
(LXXXI)	The Question Of Father Exalting	134
(LXXXII)	The Father Of Quest—Swallowing The Silence	135

NOTE:

Written in four parts, THE JOE 82 CREATION POEMS recreates the tragic, joyous, and complicated journey of a mystical consciousness through the world and time. Within its structure—based on a "free" juxtaposition of events—Wild-Man and Wild-Woman, the two personae who embody physical and spiritual nature, reveal the primordial and multitudinous levels of human experience.

THE
JOE 82 CREATION POEMS

Part 1: Magnetic Flux

I
The First Footsong of Wild-Man

        self-knowledge
          naturally
      is to put a sword
         in the
      middle of yr heart

  I am not a prophet! & I
       like the German

      students very much.
They are terrific

       says wild-man.
O give me a new good mechanical gadget
      so that I can plunge it

      in yr ViOlEnT heart!

    O sing Hanoi   Haiphong!
                          LonDon
town.
     Frank
       furt.
                the Bells of St.
       Harry
          chime!

                 like it   or not
I possess a dangerous weapon / footsong!

            sings wild-man

II
The Virgin's Baby Howling Boy Is Wild-Man's Christmas Song

      POeM
     PoEm
        one a day
make the wild man run away

    swing the iron
chain
      brake-a-back

   virtuous sent-
 iment
      crack yr neck!

   sing christmas peep!
bird-song foot / song christian snot
    rots o' ruck

   hey, the chinese are
welcomed into
        western civil-i-beast
    ATTEN 'Hut!

   And this metaphor was a wild cry
from the captive
       tit-bird's throat!
   Christmas beer christmas queer
that the wild-man
     hunched & bound 'n
  chains
     brought the quiet
 man down
      with a whim 'n a wish
make my eyes grow fascinated
      as I hear wild-man
  christmas
    song
intoning & praising

      the virgin's baby
  howling boy!

III
Wild-Man Eats Christmas Cake

      Righteousness
these are good! Birds & Fish
   Other beings (prana)
                        i p u t the j
     back (prajna)

Wild-man had Cristmas dinner today
                   Wild-man leaves
     the h out
            Yes!

Wild-man gains enlight-

        EnMENT!
   he sees the top
     of China

    spies a Christmas tree
studded with demonic ornaments
bear's green guts & eyes of Bengali

      snakè-children. Illusion
knows Me. O Joy. Christmas cake & I'm
      intent on salvation

Weapons do not break him/ H E R O heaven?
       Christmas cake.
   the single moment
             of passion
  is superior to dead 'time'

Wild-man eats Christmas cake & thrusts
     a lit candle
  at the sky.
      He screams: "He is alive!"

  A quiet breath. Compassion/
Wild-man finishes up the crumbs
   of Christmas cake.

    Quiet bliss. Obedience.
      I cannot tell thy
   Praise!

IV
Wild-Man And The Woman Of The Stony Cave

        When we come
    say the old women   we come as ugly
  as possible.
              not to give the men illusions
      of perfection   lest they stuff feathers
in their gullets

                & rage against the fate
      that sent them a wild-woman
                  wearing a wooden leg.

      O wild-man
                  smash his eye-lids
  against the picture
             of the woman with a
    mask & a wooden leg.
                    a black-eyed
st. Barbara
            vomiting up incense
  & bread
             her anger causes
the fatal
            death of farm animals/

      wild-man
          swore
    at HaLlelulYahs   &
              praises to jesus
      he thought of
    torturing the
            DIVINE MIND
    O choke on feathers!
  O choke on satan's glass eye!
    O let the hairy raging
                woman curse
the stony caves & bang her crazy leg
          of wood
    in a wedding dance!

V
Wild-Man On A Monday Nite

                    look Up
          build an altar   be sleepless
     /O Lord. Hide me near a well/   I whack
               at the mystery

      wild-man   served   God

            He ware a Holy Doktor

                              he grew near the
sea.   Beloved   or filthy dog
                                    he said.

          what am I/
                        I Am That I Am/
wild-man taught wisdom & shared his bed
                            with All.
           His fiery body
      belched golden grace/
    diamonds
 stuck on
  his/
tongue.
                  He hewed down a cross
     in his head.
                     For we are to urges
      as Satanic
                            lips/
       caress
                                baldy angels.
    I Am The Lord: I Change Not.

      Where my head points   I smear
all the doorknobs with blood/
                              grape juice
                   is so acid
                  it stings
               my lips
wild-man smiled on Monday
                  nite.
He hath smeared all the doorknobs with blood.

VI
Wild-Man Sees The Vinegar Rainbow

        vinEgar
              burns a forehead
what's the serious
              CAUSE
    did a magician do it?
                    tho/ught wild-man.
  heaven attracts
           the ordered destiny
        now separate   now come

                toGETHER
   WILD
      watermelons
              spew
ferocious blood.
          I am altogether yours—
   sings wild-man
   let me eye you   he begs

  he's like a crazy slave
                .he falls on
      his knees/
  too hard

         much much predictable pain
blood-sticky rain   making things grow
     smoothest garlic
               bulbs of the
  world.
      O Animal EYE
does wild-man belong both to

             god &
    the evil hour?
which themes speak clearest meaning?

          wild-man says:
     do you talk too much?
He sees the angel Gabriel squeeze

           —a horse head.

VII
Wild-Man Counts His Perfections

                Here he comes
           Wiping Out Evil
                            he EScapes
      to our houses
                      /exHAUSted
          he brings forth children
little climbing   insane   dwarfs
with cold lips/
           wild-man
                      says   "I want
        a virgin"
                 to spin in a dance
  her navel like a winking eye

                I suck it   & move about
    her beautiful & noble fleisch!

    Wild-man pays pennies for ritual
 & poetry
                  a bed on the black earth/
      he rests & eats cherries
     /swearing against dwarfs, dogs, U.S.
    presidents, gestures of terror, sex acts
of a SECRET SOCIETY
                  the imprint of his cock
       forced into black tar

     whatever color he loves   he eats/
  purples & fuscia   green & violet
         giggling yellows   he madly
   loves/
        he calls them stars!

      what perfection is the bone
    in my foot   what a beautiful
       day
/what is the master's name?
                I abhor the
     strength   for killing   but I Am
  a wild-man!

VIII
Wild-Man's Day B'fore New Year's Eve

        wild-man made
                Catherine die
     she defiled
           him/
                  he remembered the
      reddish haze around her head.
Christ caught between the laundry room &
              the incinerator
                       /he was doing
        earthly chores/ nor does wild-man
    remember
           the tangerine they shared each
      with t'other

                the two naked bodies
   eternalized by the sacred
                polaroid.

      he had taken pictures of her
   bent over a bundle of clean bed sheets
/smelled as pure as two bathed shepherds/
                  ass glowing near
     violet burning candles
                      .smells
of warm grape clusters/
              wild-man wearing a
     helmet & carrying the cross,
  facing the large window
                lips smiling &
     honey-gleaming
                tongue spurting
   miraculous prayer

              / his hands hold a book
     of blessings & images of golden balls
 /Christmas.
      3
    temple
         prostitutes
   sing
      praises &
 AlLeLuHiA!

IX
Wild-Man's Busted Beer Bottle

        wild-man says he hears
     the sky freeze
                he feels like a
              KING
           /it's new year's eve
                        & he knows
that he
        ALONE
              has
                  revealed
            the peacefulness of
                      the constellations

      a roach body bleeds under the
                heel of his foot/
           "once upon a time 'twas a drop
                of lust"   sings wild-man
& Now it dead & gone.
                i look away & feed
     my eye THE MOON
                    / passion PoEtRy

.standing quiet the devil opens a hole
                  i look into it/
       a filthy cuckoo book
    O wild-man cries FEAR NOT & GIRD THY
                    LOINS!

        he walks away. clasps a finger
  to a finger   tells his neighbors
        that he has tweaked the tits
     of movie stars   UNDERSTOOD THE SYSTEM

of the Universe/
              stood fascinated smelling
        the rhubarb
                    nr the sea/
    never thinking of WAR &
                floods.

X
Wild-Man's Common Truth On New Year's

                    it's significant
            that I lay open bear's head. nor do you
            protest! I do MY will.
                                Am I Not Wild-man?

                    every Hand shakes against me
                                        because of MY
                    TRUTH/
                            I speak!
                    You can trace it to Tibet.

                    once I overcame dogs racing in the woods.
            SWine taught me the Art of War / no one knows
                    my writings/
                            Did The Master have
                    ten ears?

                    I Hate poverty. Gold & jade you can
            choke on / Amber will give you a clear voice
                            You CAN SCREAM:
                    I HAVE A CLEAR VOICE!
                    You can say hairy, white, liver
                            BLACK
                                        bride with a
                    rash.
                            Still the World is not yet
                    at peace.
                                    the man walks in tar
            with his brother   Music   is   the
                    Light   going out
                                            the freeing
                    of the loved one.
                                    the Corpse has the
                    sharp/Est ears.
                    I
                        See
                            a Myriad
                                    of Evil
                                            WOrlds!
            —sang wild-man.

24

XI
Wild-Man's View-Eye Of The Blessed

            in its downward
                      (heaven)
                              course
  /yet left apart from the
                  LAST COLD
      the key to the Universe
    stood upright   in   THE   blood

        Water & fur
                    he needed
for his whole meanings
        Divine Reason
      was the Good   growth of Holy
  Plant
        completely pure
                    O Creator!
    sang Wild-man/
                I shall fulfill
 & press my hands against
              burning center.
     Death contradicts
                earth/heat/Sun
viscous damp leaf
        borning itself.

    The name rules air & fire/
  the seeking
              half monkey face/
    separating
                dry violent/
     Wounds
   the desert
              the lifted
    ancient
       Soul
         of
    /morning.
         O evil is fresh &
  without Me   —sang
     wild-man.

XII
The Birth Of Wild-Woman And/Or The Change

                    Pressed the foot
                                    on the sand
     & He/ Became
                Mother
                          Grey Water were her
                 eyes
      Thumbs pressed in   to
                           INNER BODY
              /She screamed
                         I am soft body
  My eyes are green   My Hair   is white
           what is MY Name?
                              I Play
     I Am a Great Thing   I exist
                              woman
  woman   woman   woman   pour milk for Isis
                                  Angela
                    Myrna
                              wild-woman
       Her secret
                      bells
                             flamingo singing
            lion howling
Surely tomorrow
              She will speak
                              & break twigs/
          cherries & apples fall
     to
        their
               death.   wild-woman
   smokes
          His
            last cigar
                    & laughs
      in the
            sweet morning.
                      her first day
           alive.

XIII
Wild-Woman Sharply & Triumphantly Watches

                woman is a Wild
        scientist   O Lord!   Questioning
& going forward   like a   raving nightingale
/beneath   the big-bellied   sun
                        she forces down the
    rain.
                wild-woman after her own
   swirling creation remembered   the
miracle
                  of the Nile running   indeede
    the river was faythful.
                      Full of fruit.
         she was so rational on Sunday
sitting/
        feeling her senses & passion
                        Over all
       the World
     Herself Now One
              . Unpitied.

     to be Part of Tragedy   & laugh. Watch
elephant copulate   inspiring holy love
         keeping the public
                        / at peace.
O Woman Innovator!   O Self!   O languid Messiah!

              She plucks out the weeds With
    a little finger/
                   Proud of her
gleaming Mind on the angel's head. Her
          dominion/
               & She erect
With a loud Voice
             Sings Al l
               L eLuHIA!
What Virtu is her permanence
             her Truth
  breathing out
       the sacred
            minutes/
  She grasps a voluptuous
            thighed
    Stripling

                              O an angel!
    O an angel!   & walks with him to
                          the river.

XIV
Wild-Woman & The Vegetation

      air-Boy she called him.
    He spit at her missing the frog. Paradise
   is this green front part of my Eye/   She thought he
whispered
      I rub against the slab/
            of forest Wood
    I will write my name on the parchment
  I will call myself Woman-Abraham
          my mouth uncovers
       Prayer/   Her wounds spurt milk
    Her angel
       balances
         himself with
            a Cross
    shaped in
       Water. Greed Greed Greed/
   She watched herself in the
     water

        chicken necks & backs
    glistening & turning into garlands of
  jewels from
     Babylon
          O she would flow down
the edge of
    the River
         Death grotesque & cunning
  would
    offer her money & she
         would disturb the
     water
 & shatter
    it into Flames/
       Where is the vege
     tation   I   want   to
  smell & touch
    small flowers
         . pulled wide. laughing
    Vulva.
     I am your solace!
    Sing me to my sacred grimace!

XV
Wild-Woman & The Daemon In The Water

                3 passions gave her help/
        The arrows tempted
                          the fish - - - Her
flesh risen   Over
                her sacred feet
      delightful sing   Oing.

                   Water defines
  beginning middle   & E N D

            her EYES would begin
       The pilgrimage to the C E N T E R
                            of first human
             touching fish/   a crown
 a crown a crown   & another   woman
        in the storm
                  /O false drooling
      golden-eye Demon
                afternoon fiend
     sharing a pork sandwich

                    may you drown in water.
thru love & grace may water run in your stomach sac
              pushing forth pride/
      ♯ fur coat mania
        & lechery!
      Wild-woman saw herself as Grey-beard
   for one minute   carrying a pack of gold
    & blasting a horn/
the angels running like foxes   kissing each other
    tasting the gritty chins
                meek & slipping
         in new animal shit/
    laughing & laughing *   O gleaming
   brain of woman-Abraham
                She has Made the
     devil Chop Off/ himself
                 & drink a
  cool glass of water

           . suck a little soap

XVI
Wild-Woman Sitting In The Center Of Water

                in honour of her/   the wild-woman
                              Esther of woman!
O wild star with an iron ring   eating water O she
       the graceful wizard
              /& she floats with
            Animals
                in water. She digs
     her curious
             fingers into clay. Clay cries

           thou Art the criminal! See what
light splits beneath shadow.
          Big Shit Fish Gives no warning—
  when it turns around your snatching hands!
O cry fish   stop!   smile your eyes
    10,000 times so that the fish
  lick her face   /sweet.
                  wild-woman
          Saw the Profound Cave
     it has no beginning to the beginning
   it has glory in its thirsty opening/ no greater
  laughter
          than the cracking shoot of light/
             O nature of light!

There she found no retribution   No burning of green
          plant & fish
                         Sound handed
       & walking to her   everything
  feeling like the yolk of an egg.
                    what is
       religion? fishes shaking
    in her blood
              /her Mind
    linked   To   THE
           brittle & ancient
         fish-trap   foul
     reeking leather.
  Her lawful Spirit.
               Her on the edge
       of earth.
  O Wild-woman sitting in the Center!

XVII
The Judgement In The Water And Song

                      does wild-woman say
      I AM DEAD   separated/   dancing
in the water   leaving swill for
          fish. Gurgling & jeering sea-
monster of killing   .intelligence. O
TIME   s a n c t i f i e d
                              & swirling!

                        the breath is complete
        & ferocious
                    forced back
        into
      the
      human heart/ my old king
of the void   gulped boiled
            milk   & painted
pictures of sea-dragons & landscape
      . died of rocks piled
    around
    his throat/
                in all directions
wild-woman saw the skill of walking on water
          the fins
        suspended in green plants
      /red obsessed mouth of fish.
   O what is in back
 of my
skull!   What makes a sound behind
    the brain?   my veins are
       pink flowers
/fleshly unchained ornaments
   shine.   O it is my life!   Beware
sea-monster above all I smell you! O proof is
ugly green skin in the water. O wild-woman had many
 judgements/ laws against the
Air.
               this mollusk society absolves
      human punishment & there is
    /no blame only lungs swelling with
  Air. O wild-woman's body
 sang
      with air!

XVIII
Wild-Woman & The River & Moon

                        black swan's eye finds
    the crown   -   -   -   seed
                                named the point
            of blue. Sun/
                              water
what is the pity in water? where is the line
    of the shore?   The thing of life goes
       forward
                          The butterfly
  is ever moving, glistening, sucking air

                music is gleaming
        the stars of tissue & wood
 . mollusk blood
               surrounding the root.

wild-woman her grief is tearing   .into paradise.

            rock is dry
          & turning
               reaching
            the energy
        of river/

            fingers
                     the
          leaping clean
        nakedness of self!

so Sing! what is the beginning of the
              story? children without
     names. I drew the Sun/ I Saw!

Lastly   she   sees   the

dark.   electric body flickering in wisdom
      O what then?   Today.   hatred
 of water   or   maddened stone/
       fish twined river bloom
    /magic of morning   &
    gathering plants.
                  wonder of the
       human face.
    O who is king?
            the moon.

XIX
Wild-Woman Beholds The Sea's History

        devouring the mountain &
   dancing when all the singers, the shell-
fish, the organs of speech say, semen
catch & enchant the utterance of king
          &
        W A T E R

  in the same time wild-woman justified the
beats of praise & thanks the first born myth
  of Evil   father of mollusk
    killed the stars breathing
   flame hooking into the body

  Is love new? where is sea-weasel? where is
the mask of listening? O what is possible here?
lower the rock
give yesterday's
slime to
memory
   & this   the   r i c h e s t
       mud.

O laughter fulfills the flying sea-horse Ha-ha! Ha!
   the glimmering strange knees of
  water-horse ---the beauteous strange!

       in this new water-field
  exist the layers of God's raving history hand on
his own thigh, Jehovah hand on her own breast, Jehovah
   when peace comes to the water.

   B E H O L D T H Y S E L F!

  from the spirit I have friends, says
  the wild-woman the lumps of fish I eat
  sustain the world my flesh so beautiful my
   body shines at the moon.

        mollusk thou art so wise!
   let us weep together in the
   front
  of the
world

                drink
         sweat   No, thou cannot
      sweat!
    forever the water cools.

XX
Wild-Woman In The Sea In The Long Day

                    chanting fish say, cuckoo!
      Look a whale between human beings, a night of spring!
    the flowing of yesterday/ the dream in the coral gourd
                —a strange level
              for herself to hear. Brown
        pain of dying fish, leafless ugly
      terrible sweetness   O death-rigid
                 horror that flies
around my head!   Sometimes the snow fell on
                the River, wild-woman called,
      Don't break/ O fly softly down &
  be swallowed up/   the River is cool
          & young.

                            the tail weighed as
                much as a
            banana
        leaf.
      a song/
     a cry
   of
  the fall/
ing Sun.   Black behind silver - - - the water
                          blossom
              the wandering away
            the sleep of the snow
         O forever!   Suddenly the 5th moon
     & bitter sea-weed
    & giant loving
   mollusk &
  the morning's sun-
 ray perfectly white
gave wonder & scattering &
  Song &
 breath &
finish.   the victory
             in water-language.
        in Sky.
                  in Sky.
            in Sky.
        in the long Day.

XXI
The Judgement Of Water

                          riotous is the
                black water, the body & the continent
    Holy   . . . glory   . . . is the good
fruit. Amen.   your mind is the discipline of god/ the man
                denies the sweetness of
                            W A T E R
      the silent ness of   life. Who keeps the
precepts   the mildness   of   doves?
                            O all rebirths
        come under emptiness/ the Essence
   the suck of vital Air
                b r e a t h
            passion/   of lung
        the five darknesses
                     intellect of
        ear, nose & tongue
   the skin of the past & future
                    the ether
of purity
    & Experience
           .Me.   O wild-woman
  My worshiper
             .give devotion
      to the she in the world/
   Shekinah   thou art
favorable
    in
      my
        eyes.
               & the wind makes
the earth turn dry.   love in one place of fire.

       the tremor
     of the
   living
     particle
   of God's
blessing.
              where is the fiend of killing?
    for I know it is pure this death in
  water/   stink sublime killer fish
 First whale of banishment!   O unrighteous
                      water-snake!
    O Punisher!

XXII
Wild-Woman And The Truth In The Water

                    rain & waiting   bowing,
biting starfish, mollusk, I tell you — says
the wild-woman, what crazyness there is in the sea
                you must hold your ears
            hard   &   drift   away.
    close by rocks
      the tail-fins
  of a little
god
  . in victorious water.   Blessed strong water/
      it satisfies
      the
      world/
  hair is so beautiful stroking
the
    River.
        where are the
      oysters?   are they
    spinning close by?
        my desires!
      the gorging frogs
are my desires! Praise be! O Praise!

I have gathered powerful dreams shining thru
      the time of summer. death is breathing
on the sea stones
    daylight
    the opening of the lake
  says, my breath is   poetry
the process of the earth is eating/
      shimmering
    fish-lip
  obscene ecstasy
of dying fish
/the golden sky of heav'n is
wailing.
      pity the poor lengths
    of dying
  fish, the infected
  sickening color of
green. O water & blood gushes hard
    from her side!

Part 2: The Enfolding

XXIII
Wild-Man In The Fascinating Forest

                              come out against the
                earth   thief   6 thousand dumb worlds
connect with the gleaming soul/   Adam's fall is
                    a beam of light
            . o suck the mud   & do this
            & that. root around   &   burn
        beneath the sun.   to the first hill
& I see the throne!   Who sits? Where is the scream?
                . There is no singing
                   surrounding me.
                                    The Eagle
            describes
                       the Judgement/   dark/
                       unredeemed
                       process of
            stink & rotting
                                    O this walking to &
                fro   astonishes!   & if the bread
            sweats blood   is that
                        not a
                        miracle?
        The skin of the tree   is the bark   the
    bark of the man   is the skin
                                        /I have waited for
                the end   I, Wild-man, put my hand
                    on the left side
            of Eternity   & kiss-off the old fashioned
         stars!   cuckoo!   yipee!   where is your strength?
Have you seen the rays of light?   The bang of lightning
            does   violence to the birds!   it Shatters
            s h a t t e r s   Shatters
                           the Holy skulls!   I vomit up
            eggs.
                            kiss me father for dragging
                    me out of the w a t e r
                                        & flattening out
                        long & still
                           my feet   so   that   I   may
            stand
                                    in the forest.
                        You never broke your word you
            Heavenly System Maker!   You have let
    me make noise on the land!
                                    Between my teeth
                    I sing your name!

XXIV
Wild-Man In The Gethsemane Of The Forest

       Jacques
       Jack
       John
        Jon
   a than jonathan Jacques
   Augustine all knowledge is consecration
shit of the bull   Creation   where is the Mother
    the Angel
        the erotic
     Jewish geographer   Our Father
  climbs the tree
   & dips his
 peepee
     into his
own
   pheno Man!

        O when wild-man leant against
  the bush & here it went crackling near his head
O the bush spoke Without any sound & he became
      sore afraid/
     Thus the first prayer was in the He
    brew & with zeal wild-man study'd
  the Holy language
         /a part of the   green-
      jealous   o the whirling world
   rejected the piety . of the first wild-man/

      Consider when you enter upon
  the Scripture
    & you recite it well the shit
  of the bull has two outstretched finger-
  prints pressed into the shit/ O the singer!
     the author!
    the happiest Roman
  dancer!
         . the Forest
   holds Grace   no unnatural desert
    & big-assed camel
   & flying bug
  that eats up the fruit.

O always the earth endures the rendering   the fat making
                the yowl   of   the hound
                        of heaven
            the
            YES
            NO!   the possessed /God.

XXV
Wild-Man & The Temptation In The Forest

                                                  to learn everything
                          the V   of the sun   springing
  & did it die afterwards?   the Lord God made the heav'n
              & the earth
                               what matters
      if a kid does not seethe in its mother's milk!
  & the glass   is the dream   interlocking with
        the fire   from   the sand   it owes
            its genus/
                      O wild-man ate up
        a fig   from   an egyptian
            dancing girl's
      hand/   Sweet one!   he called out.

       this stage   is explanation   proving
   the unequal steps   taken   by our big-footed
        elders.
              O I am the Grand Explorer!

   & then he took a big pot & laid it down
   on the ground & let the blood from
      the rhinoceros
                  plop swiftly &
    surely & let it gush &
    flow as niftily as
      the water from
      His side!

    whosoever believeth in me On my Name
    is as the wind blowing thru the grass.
        & so jumping between leaves
          & roses & cat
      turd/   he pondered on the land of His
  captivity/
           & stuck his hand twixt his
     green thighs & Lo!
    ----- the thighs were quite dry!

                      up sprang the herbs
  & up the green corn (O like His thighs!) &
  up the seeds & the humans &
      St. Victor & the false

                    Jewish one &
                    the Correct
                    one & all
                    that
                    squirm
         on the ground.   O Lord, salvage mine iniquities!
O Lord, if it please thee!

XXVI
Wild-Man In The Essence Of The Forest

```
                              destined      He
          the material     his Holy Individual      Sun
    I have no pain!     He cried     I    &    Mine!
                         I am as a convert     before I
                   was Saviour         a 6 month
             creeper in the grass!
                                    this Urge      is
              Zeal     it increaseth    like the pleasures
    in the world.         The eternal birth    &    laughter!

                 O side by side wild-man rocked
                   hisself & swallowed a fruit or a flower
              a thistle, clover & a vine, a this meat or that
         fish, a that water & this wine, all the nature of
                nature       He SAW    in his trance
```

                    it swirled
                    in his spleen
                    it whirled
                    in his gut
                    it skipped
                    in his blood
                    it whacked
                    in his fat
                    it shook in
                    his lymph
                    it stank in
                    his piss
                    it laughed
                    in his grease
                    it jumped in
                    his pus
                    it kissed his
                    marrow &
                    grimaced at
                    his sorrow
                    it sneered
                    & howled
                    at the origin
                    of the world
   & so on & forth!
                                       where is the wealth?
                 is it a moth?   my body Act?   my own
                    strange light?   my hair?   my food
               in my Holy Digestive Tract?   my peacefulness?

                my snot?   my sighs?
             my eyes?   my spit?
          my   all   things   my
    pure self?

XXVII
Wild-Man In The Terror Of The Forest

                      this woman   where?
It's enough, I'm dead. No, I'm not!   I'm
doubling & doubling with life, I'm blazing I'm
shining   forth   forth   forth
                                      O I'm
        standing on my legs!   How happy!
     How happy   what a show
           I Am
                 that I Am

               I AM THAT I AM!   I speak
out of the essence   of the bliss   I
last forever
                            My manhood!   O my
       Legs! My palms!   They
   make psalms
           about
               my
                  palms!
                            Song testifies
       to my wondrous thighs!   Ah lalalalala
la   la
   la   lalalala
        la! Hallelujah!
                        & all the rest!

if I succeed in catching all new things   what of old
     stuff?   What about the first
              confession
      of
        my
          mighty
                g u s h i n g
    cock?   Have ye heard it shout?
Have ye seen its black eye?   Have ye seen
  it   face   to   face
                          Indeed
      you can
     credit to wild-man
       the   whole   fuckin' Human Race
  /with its joys 'nd torments; apples &
  betrayal
        /silent & chewing
     giggling & praying
                  /crying

    with a terrified
/spasm
                /breaking the bonds.

XXVIII

Wild-Man In The Reversal Of The Terror

        if I succeed in catching all new things
    what of old   stuff?   what about
        the first confession
                      of my mighty
     gushing   O g u s h i n g
cock? &
   have
      ye
        heard
           it
           shout?   Have ye seen
   its black eye?   Have ye seen it
face to face
        O indeed ye can credit
    to the Wild-man   the hole
fuckin' Human Race
          /with its joys 'nd
      torments; apples & betrayal
        /silent & chewing
         giggling & praying
   /crying
     with a terrified/ O a spasm!
/breaking the bonds.
           this man   where?
  it's enough, I'm dead. No! I'm Not!
O I'm doubling & doubling with life, I'm blazing I'm
    shining   forth forth forth forth
                       O
                   I'm
standing on my legs! How happy! How happy I Am
                that I Am!
     I AM THAT I AM! I speak out of the essence
of the   bliss   I   last   forever

                  My manhood! O MY
           Legs! My Palms! They
      make psalms about my palms!
     Song testifies to my wondrous thighs!
  Ah lalalalallalalala
             la la
                 la Hallelujay-yay!
       & all the rest!
                  Alleluiah!
       /O Praise!

XXIX
Wild-Man & The Dream On The Forest-Edge

```
                        disappeared        & the flies!
        shutting the mouth quickly
                            the human being's
                            mouth Eyes
                    struggling
                Apart/ O Away!
        from
Death.        all my possessions/ except wisDOM
                    blood-the-ocean       speaks
                backwards        URine
        & the smart-alecks
        & all the highest souls        induce the trance
                    /if it kills        you
        Peace! & Be With Thee!
                                    round the forest
                    stuffing the
                    wood/ up/against/
                the one Always
                Principle
                glands & Water      I can create
        the Lion's Leg/ brave & beautiful I
        bless my Eyes with stones
    /my low cries      say to the      monsters
            Lo    Look   Around!    I believe that
        the Night/time is in peril
    at midnight something    the monkey without the
                    legs      jumps on midnight's
                back/    sometimes I ripped open
                a cloud & made stream
            in my Sacred nostrils
            the Smoke         a dream's a dream

                    O wild-man bowed Up/d
                                    o
                                    w
                                        n & jumped
        & saluted his own Round   Thighs   His head
                            moving on a   r i v e r
                        of yellow gold
                    He said: My own tooth
                    feels so    s i l k y
```

                                I will
                   suck   up the
                   elixir   good-good!
         of the   rose   after I piss
    on the bank
of the River.

XXX
Wild-Man Speaks From The Nest Of Birds

```
                        Suppose you run     after
            so many good         fruits.  / I have
    SpoKen          O not the Deadly requirement
                 of fat-suck-a-worm Righteousness!

                     But
                      I
                  mean scrupulous love/
                        tree    dewdrop    the
               whole underneath of the   Moon      just
                 consider
                      the Exertion of
                            Prayer
                  the knees give themselves &
             seek the ground to sleep       the breath
           has no fear         for once    it finds a
          sweet-fit    the art of the breath-again   O
            root of Reason &    holy Function/  is simple
        is not arrogant      is Wisdom     O thanks!

                          wild-man
                       wild-man eat a
                        drop
                        of the
                    meat that looks like a
                    jewel     the head of a
                    birdling     little hideous tongue
                    cherishing    its death    O free body!
                if I pronounced the World    Be Small!    a great
             er form of Heaven          Song near The Sweet Hole
                         In The Sky          heaven is
                         old Divine! Wondrous!
                      the Great Sea Of Laughter! Hoggle! Hoggle!
               o       g
           H       g       l
                          e!    the loving world!
                                            the beasts
                                         of delicious
                                            Scents!
                                  the  fierce grass
                              warm in Sun/
                         lite-Holy.
```

XXXI
Wild-Man Talking On The Nature Of His Form

                      belonging   seeing the soul
/twisting/   the soul   like   false   it was false
topped with poison   evil milk   the heart of mother
                   Worst-love   the jet
       of her blood   debauch! debauch! debauch!
                    —in her blood!

              O where is Wild-man driving!   what
Power is thrown on top   of Him/   is his
11th experience death-looking? giving   disappear!

           here it is
           manifest
           fuck the mind
/east to west/ see
           the rose
           & drop your
           nose   let
           it slide on
           the delightful
                 vision!
   my stomach especially   is a beast, says the
wild-man   almost 20,000 times it cried for
         yellow   —   I sing for love!
 I am sustained!
  The large middle stone
 is amazing!
              It is a thousand year old brain
          /hardened into a diamond
         / O never call it a mouth
         it is different
                   —hear! hear!
 I fly to the south
 & I sing for love!
              the animal   sniffs
           the vegetation
         the kidneys flush the nation
               O all is not lost
    what is dirty color?
    where is my extra tail?
               Lo & Behold!
        Wild-man leads all the rest.
  if I looked into the River I would see his gigantic
nostrils! Selah!

XXXII
Wild-Man Names A Creature & Calls Water-Bright!

                                                      miles   away   the sand
    mad-going   Your wisdom   DOM! DOM! crosses
                                                over to the   bar bar i an
River.   Even to men
                          &
                  birds. Fidelity.   what a middle
             to the past   the fire   the raging petals
/ c o m p a s s i o n   who will go
                              to HELL
                       for what crime?   & smiles
   between friend & friend
        eating from
           one
            wooden bowl.   Dip the feet into
        bright water / WATER-BRIGHT!   wild-man called
a Great Duck   WATER-BRIGHT!   Dog-yowl is the
                 world, said He the wild-man/
             Dog-yowl
          is the
          written word
          unwritten   take the flower   split up
   the 40 purple Suns   count the excellence
                                             /Sound Gongs!
                      WATER-BRIGHT!
                      crying Dog!
                      WATER-BRIGHT!
                      WATER-BRIGHT!
              YOWL-DOG!   O sweat scream!
Perfect Truth   coagulate!   HardEn!   S
                                                        p
                                                         r
                                                         i
                                                         n
                                                       g out!
             in love   the
       gradations   /like Perfect Salt
                Listen, Listen!

          LaLaLaL l llalala
             La l
                     la   /break pots!
            dance stones!
          touch the light!
                      I face myself
                 & sing!

XXXIII
Wild-Man And The Influence Of The She

                                      his Torture
         divides   With all Temptation/   All creatures
there singing
               &
          &   &
            &
          &   r w n
          &   g o i g O growing by force, power
of
   the
      groin!   wild woman with hanging breasts!
                the bloody intensity/   the dance
        of veins   spleen of the wedding
    party/ the masked Sun   dragging the Virgin
the
  woman of birds, rubbing her stomach with
                         pitch/cutting her
               hair
            & forcing her to èat
        /it did   haunt her/
     the naked wylde   birds. He Saw.
Wild-man
     walked into the
               wilderness
                       the
       w
        i
        l
         d
          e
          r
         ne
          ss
  Spoke.   He swayed.   he
      hid like a beast
         he sucked herbs & embraced a
    tree   he tore out
  his   swaying-red   liver
/he dwelled   in   the woods/ & layed
down   next to his/bride   her braided
    hair tasting of plants.

XXXIV
Wild-Woman & The Invention Of Life

                        the words
                 are   in
          the eggshell   piece of hair &
  the first part   of all   /this is nothing
  widespread
breath on the dead/
with the edge of the nose
    Sun/Head   the dog   ha-ha
    grows/
                        when wild-woman blew
             the snail to the   one-sixteenth
       point of Astonishment   O Joy Was Fire!

    space between
    two, in the
    drop of water.
    clear & Join
      the time
        time
        time   with Many Laws   of the good
 the pride   of   alTeR/ing the teeth of
                the Moon.   the grain of
                the sea
            the texture
         of fish-skin
        the prayer
      of   Water/Lord!   who is WATER-BRIGHT!
  the   beginning meeting   with
      the man.
  what is the wild boar?
          On a morning   the Left side
     of
      the faithful creaTures   was filled/With
 magical germs
         God-blown Out   in an Idea
      & wild-woman
            on her compassionate feet/
 green-Wisdom Lighting Her Eyes

   the identity/
      the Sacred language   kissing wood blood
              hocus pocus
         manacled & existing
     eating up the flying gold
    threads of   the light.

XXXV
Wild-Woman & The Song From The Breast

                                    Head so full
                  of Amazement!   from   joy   to   joy
         in herself
                            the
                        glittering   b e a u t i f u l
               3rd   prayer   raging   then
                 her
              skin
            like
         raindrops   blue-alive   life!   the
                         tender
                        haunting
              -      b r e a s t   /of the sea-bird
                        dripping d
                                  o
                                wn
                                  o
                                w
                                  n dow
                                       n &
                 the rock is picked   the rock is picked
               the rock is picked   /it is to be gotten
       to live.   to live.
                                    none too great
                         brush   hair   around   the
                     teeth
                                        where is the sad
                              ness
                   of cutting   the-fish   for-food
          corn-grain   white-bird   water-BRIGHT!
         struggling hour   & the fire-torch!   bitter-leaf/
                               big   face   great
                          breast-Song
                       body-shine a sparkling lily
                         blood-lovely
                         woman-lovely
                     horse   grows   horns.
                                  sounding dark after/
                        the mating.

58

XXXVI
Wild-Woman And The Wonder Of Fat, Honor And Death

                                                      Then set the created colors
      /above   the stone   spirit

                 freedom?   ?   ?   what binds the
           lake?   only the self   we
     have a body   said the wild-woman Supreme shell/
Is   the   cracked/truth   that is the way of annihilation
             Emptiness only
            is   nostril-breath skull-song
     love of the strange laugh on earth
    pointing feet   the heart exhausts
      the flowing world/

                       and if/ the
        single
      first   month of   the
    year   singing breath
    /eating   rice flesh fruit   The Master
kill! kill!
                  what of the
        teaching?
         the   dust?   the
    drifting
     bare   living   Air/fish/Happy

the two clear things   in water   are they Mad?

what is the cover of   it?   the top is the sky/
                   the dog bone
                      says   bite mouth!

       metal
       earth
       wood
       skin
       fat
       honor
       death
       dove   is   food

                      grow   Book
            of Screams   the
         mild   Wonder
       is everLasting
  /all Praise!

XXXVII
Wild-Woman & The Joy Incantation Song

                                          laughter
            she loves peace   first/ watching the rebirth
quick breakaway   the soul is called!   Hehahehah!   wat
               a wonder   the plucked
                          smell &   sound
          maybe the earth is   for pleasure
   watch the skin of the earth!   it should not suffer

            many wars
            & laughing   Her
            everywhere   eat milk
            pull fur
            drop the stone
            let fall it hard
            slit the nose
            & burn the turd
            make the law
            & wink the Eye
            say, "eternal"
            & lick the thigh
            jump the bum
            & love of God
            create He them
            suck wisdom hard
            fall down fast
            & sing all around
            give a penny
            & quick pass gas
            none of this is false
            or true
            say howdedoo
            to Hanging jew
            save me save thee
            save ye & Fred
            save mish save mosh
            & THAT drop dead
            O this is holy
            & that's my name
            I smell sweet self
            & burn the flame!
            Thou dwell thou dwell
            O world of being
            I tell I tell
            thy sacred singing!

                            O World (Yes)
    Thy feet   are graced with everything!

XXXVIII
Wild-Woman & The Shine Of Thought & Talk

```
                        one attachment one funct
                   ion              THAT Nature
       /light    self    like a black distance
   the point      separated     when each
feeling      How it is full        power!   burns &
                                                 moves
                                              and
                                          full    power
                                      and
                                  in the rock      laughs!
                    hahehha
                       ha
                         hah    he
                              he      .Som.
                  I would have wood    growing     in
       my teeth   So I would be the Oldest &
    The Strong     est.   So.    I push
   forth the       speech     right thing going
 .sleep.  home. Som.
                     I think my hand wants to sing!
              Live in the mud. Smell the meat      from
   Hope.       yesterday       I put a lid
    from           the jackal    on top
       of my.      Skull.    I roll
              around the place
                  where. I
                     piss
                        think that the Ripe Human
                 gives his Eyes    to you      Sweat
         a          dream     out       of the
                        face in the Sky
                              Long
                 touch        and the works are
         hundreds and thousands    all grass is the same
      jackals      blacker     than  the night-time Sun!

                    O in your belly
                    is a bean
                    the many forgotten
                    black hole
                         scene
                     So blow on your
                     chin & drink
                     from the drain
                     The man transformed
```

       is the man the
            same   So
      dinkydoo & dovey don
      let loose your knees
      & scream to the Sun!

XXXIX
Wild-Woman & The Leaping Ape

                                      So when there were
        58,000   impulses   I and Mine &
            Magic   the killing
         nature   /On death   is
              Ocean
                                      distant
/Oil hanging from the   mouth.
                                the
                                praise
                                of Life/
                                light
                                Silken
                                I Am Not
                                this   flower
                                The Order
           is the Singing Aperture
                                the
                                  hole
                    of
          holy   Noise

       pure   self   is   passion
/the leaping Ape
drinks from the Shore
     dur-up!
     dur-dup!
        Earth   Slants/
          To My Lips!   Ape Speaks!

              So Silent So Red
           the Energy   the Active
   Supreme
       idea   O Sun the tongue
Compassion!
           without looking round
     I Move
  in the evening
   the evening
          I find the/ Music
      the entrance
        to the touch   Awakeness!
   all Praise/ Drink!

XL
Wild-Woman In The Middle Of The Hanging Tongues

blood is/
fishes viscous sacred Again Always
repeated   its Form Again Over is Ever running About
at Will is Will & Filling without ceasing is
Fear   to   Stop!   That stops
nourishment   is   Dead!
O What Miserable
is nothing no
Pride
in the world of darkness.
Glum-Song! Glum-Song
stinking weep-
song! drip-
song! never be anymore! O Woe!

we are dancing naked
out of the cave inta inta
reeking stink cold
world! O Yes!
Naked I
brung
only the
hopping hope to not be
afflicted
that nothing would
spurn my choppers & Maw
that creatures
would fall
in a Stupor at my killing
blows, that I Exist over
the hanging tongues
O My Enemies!   May they be weaker than Me!
May the
first Joel write a prayer
about my Energy
may the idea
of human d i g n i t y begin with
my own
salvation
my virtue
my glory
my not being a
VILE WORM   but I

carry nothing Out
Except the Flaming Torches
—held in my hands!

XLI
Wild-Woman & The Taste Of The Wisdoms

```
                                        the realization
         in itself      Own Love      it is done it is to
         be Done!  the
                   appeal
                   of the
                   blind
                   ecstasy!    the hoopla doctrine      not of
         Mind         but     of     the gentle eye (Who?) & So
                            Wild-Woman
                                        by the bounds
                                    of Speech       the bounds
                                   wished Away!  Grace
                                 leaps like a roe
                                 on the Unbegotten
                                 back of the Oil-
                                 fingered      the    destroyer. the Sun
         Says          Joy     Is     To     Come!
                                                        if that
                                    the finite    the growing the
                            Daughter the Person is given
                                                    the stripe
                                        is perfection   the
                                    color
                                    the rock    the possible
                                   the revolving the      Home
                          under grass      the drink    near   the
                         good.  Our Air.   O Look I See the snow-white
         Rose.      the form
                    of the body
                    treats the
                    reality
                           the        love      is     peace      full
         strike              &         be       new-borne    &
                                  that you              notwant  to
                                   notwant          to
                                   desert
                                  the One
                                 the Salt!
                                         Secrets!     the spirit the
                                    fresh      instant
                                   the foretaste    of    the 3
                                   Wisdoms the
                                   Life in the Hold
                            of the Blood & So I Am       Glorious
```

XLII
Wild-Woman & The Premonition Of Technology

          bring out the iron!
   consider   what the dark member is?
the blown-monster cheeks! O, does a Soul Come Out?
        the blessed souls?
          reversed from death?
      freee? freee?
           According to the
  fixed   visible   Order /thou hast forgotten
         the Music of
        CrEaTiOn
          whirl in the dust
          blow in the rust
          ram your teeth
in the greasy crust!

         the area from a star
       to Ethiopia   inhabited
  /is 2 Zones   2 beasts dance out

            from the
     Danube River to the humans
  who
       go
       beyond
       the   twelve regions
     of   life/ where is the iron?
 to the moon &
    a name/   Wild-woman
       saw the Creator
           pure &
           clearest
           calling it
           Mind
           the
           Mother
           fabulous
          the sky to
          the earth
          the same way
/to iron to mud to concrete to   aluminum to
       the waning ooze of petroleum &
   the injured

                        hand o' human
                       what is the first
    Scientific   Solid Ball
                            /iron circle!

XLIII
Wild-Woman & The Second Moment Of Science

                      & the Naked direction   the
shape
Force
Black
Spirit
          talking & finding   in the dim   'Thou'
the forest   the   bullet   the   eye   of   rimmed
      meaning   & So threatening &
            pressing

              from where the world filled   Sound!
       Speech/long sparking   the roots beside
                  the Heart!

                           & the nut
                           & the gear
                           & the knuckle
                           & the
      knife!   the stick!   the box of blood
                        the hill suffused with
                        star-Voice!

      & then what pressed into human life   bulging
            six Urges!   beautiful revealing &
              listening!   & 8 darknesses
              burn & chant!

        I Suck Metal!   I put
                      Lead on my
                      Head
                      I drop oil
                      on my
                      Soil
                              I whisper I
        am Wild-woman I hear
                      that robbers
            see visions   of   crowning
      possibilities!
                    so soft
                    Radio what
                    is Witness
                    what smells
                    Floor wax
                    what hears
                    I.B. mussel

Hey, Vat means ziz technical brotherhoog?

XLIV
Wild-Woman & The Naming Of Metal

                         & Yes this practice & THAT question
        this what?   the inner
                         meat of purification
             O made clean!   is the
          drifting liver/   O sobbing gland!

       & then borne on the eastern side of the
  worlde   falling lower & lower
                     soil begets
                     metal/ Again
                     Female names
                     the   oyl

                  power is the
         Pleasure Answer & Again
             /it is named METAL

      the ancestor had the blessings of the Great Wood
(God?)   as found on the wall
               the worship   the first shot-gun
                              the memory

                of name & VICTORY
                               born into
      the world today   the cut hair & the finished
  time   of   nature
                  the warmth of boiled meat
           the Silence   before the flowers
              O draw up the legs & marvel
         at   REALIZATION

                Steel
           copper bronze
               lead
              medicine do not fail
        to be excellent!
                   the instructions
  from the Bureau of Cosmos! the storehouse
           skin, flesh & bones
        lightly into harmony
      Atoms & greed
    lust for   p u r e   l a n d
                       true RAPTURE
       meat/STEEL

Part 3: Fire Clay

XLV
Wild-Man & The Peeking Into The Cloud

        the Celestial

  point.

         from
         this Region
  we have been speaking

         but we plunge
      into the earth
    we drink the gas every day of the moon.
The marks in the

      sKy   claim Possession

     the privilege is the
completely PURE
      distinct Soul in life & death.

   only 3 points lie   separate!

      eyes & nose

  /mouth calls IMPULSE!

        Wild-Man dreamed &
    was taught I WILL TEAR AWAY

           marks between
the gaze the vision the pall the sleep the truth the
clouds the ivory the virtue the dubbed the sub-
stantial the word the place the marking the
movement the ideal the age the decline
the new the strength the year the
law the jaw the five the mean
ing the fires the quicken
ing the narrow the hole
the heaven the smell
the eyes the soul
the Ocean the
eternal the
biting
the
        it is beyond us.

XLVI
Wild-Man & The Righteous Perspective

                          I found the Mohawk Valley
    singly   Wild-Man!   He participated in
  staggering   discovery   (shoot-his-mouf-off)
                     Oil I have found
           Cumbustion I have made!

     whatever the Sun bleaches is   History

ripening apples   faceless Father!

          white Sulfer speaks perpetually
   thousand say single   intelligence   shit of the
 Mohawk flying crow   the burnt word   the
                      Singing Name
      but to say that there are
    kindnesses!   the horse is
leaping & there is a record of
the Motion   Full Sun
 receives   && is   turning black
the dream of perfection

                what belongs?
                what holds?
                what takes us up here?
                what is oil-mortal?
                what is Natural
                envelopment?
                what is O explain!

       brilliance under the
  Sun.   the   limit
    has left the last
  cold
  /breast rib stomach Sighing hurr/
icane

                  Woman where is Wild-man?
 water unites earth
        the created things
      understanding
     No Numbers!
   begotten
    cubes   rustle   Hear!
existence forever.

XLVII
The Funnel Of Steel In The Green Forest Bush

                        Smiling so that between
      the Skull   this hour waits   is magical &
Swinging Forward! My Soul!   My Soul!

                       underneath the tree
     most fabulous judgement   the gleaming branches
in the shape of   blood-bright   forever
           beginning   /a mountain of
     lead   colder than   a blue sky

              Hum-Ho!
            pipe o' iron
         a funnel of steel
       a shaft of rusty alum
         iNum tardy-tar &
         feather yr bum
  sing Allel & tivili Tum! sing Allelu & tivili
TUM!

              the course to the
       earth   beauty-slow & back
  ward.   the duration
      of the dark body of human

what if I asked if your eyes were healing all that
    was suspended above?
                  my blue of my revealed
           breaths O Staring &
   laughing instinct! O Shape of the Snake
& all that is moving
           closer/

     the voice
     falls   it is coming
     into being
     it is   Always Found
     it curves Without the burning/
     all Moon in hope!
     /what smell of the moment
     is a color?
     what is the texture
     of the good
     /eternity

what is the Name of Singing from
the Green Forest Bush?

XLVIII
Wild-Man & The Rhythm Of The Mechanized System

                          who belongs   Devout
            thousand rebirths   mix
                            a few seeds
                            three days
                            thick at the top
  how do these plants digest   in full Sun/

                6 submarines
                fast frigates
                1 battalion   one onion
              12 fast roses & a shower of s p e e d i n g
  meteors   1 reconnaissance squadron   15 minesweepers

                helpless in
                the line of duty a
                man dies
        head sticking out of cement
     /it's a thrilling once-in-a-lifetime-
spectacle!
              suck rubber & chop timber
       /steel plants   & the coming
Afrikanization of 12 hens & 24 cheeses/ O Boy!

            a man with ideas
            & a man whistling
            in the light/tyme
            of revolution
            & bloody experience/

                         What about the
          equipment
what about the fish   throw them back in the Sea.

                while the
                gap
                could
                lead
                to
            Fearing Things

        O Motor Vehicle
        O Radio Station
        O Meat & Wool
        O Major Airline

             O Sacred Mechanized
          System
    o' bliss!

XLIX
Wild-Man & The Overhearing Of Disasters

                                        in India & Kenya
                snails & slugs, moss animals   lewd
  Aardvark, rhinoceros   Baboon Polar Bear
                      /all creatures with heads
           severe with wave lengths of
     radiation
                      moved 1 square foot
                      moved 1 square inch
                      moved 1 square T O N G U E

            over the world's surface
       much of the land has been devastated by
     reckless lumbering & chronic killing
/Savage burning   uprooting more & more
              O Epidemic
              O Earthquake
              O Fire
              O Flood
              O Eruption
              O Storm
              O Cyclone
    O B U B O N I C   P L A G U E!

                     where's Rome?
            fire!
        where's plague?
      jumping hot!
   what's a shock to the human system?
 The Black Death!
what's an Atomic disaster?
Hiroshima!
                what's a hot seat?
              Electric chair!
           what's a mine disaster?
        Suffocation!
                          where's the
             future?   peace propped
                         up on its
                         head!
          in atmospheric
          chemistry
          the danger to Earth's inhabitants

  /is feared   dead meat dyed pink!

               have a drink of black
          water   it will take but
     a few minutes

L
Wild-Man & The Bad News Telegram

                            life will take but a few
    seconds/   have a drink of
        black water
                              dead meat dyed pink!

    danger to Earth's inhabitants is feared!

in atmospheric chemistry   where's the future?

           peace is
           propped
           up on its
           head

suffocation is a mine disaster
   the   electric   chair   is   a
      HOT SEAT

    Atomic disaster is an
    event   at Hiroshima
    the   Black Death   is a
    shock to the human system
    plague is jumping hot!
    fire is burning Rome
O BUBONIK PLAGUE   is not wonderful

        Cyclone O
        Storm O
        Eruption O
        Flood O
        Fire O
        Earthquake O
        Epidemik O

      land is devastated by lumbering industries
      & chronik killing/
Savage burning
        snails & slugs & moss animals &
     lewd Aardvark, rhinos   & some Baboon
   polar bear/ all creatures with heads severed
 & oozing wave lengths of radiation

                                        moving 1 square
                                foot.
                                        moving 1 square
                                inch.
                                        moving 1 square
                        tongue.
        in India & Kenya & U.S.A. & over the whole
worlde's surface   disaster.

LI
Wild-Man & The Memory Of The Dying Poet

```
                              to prevent a communist
            victory                 confront the tribal
  elder                         check his level of
                    literacy
                                & after a murderous
                      flash-flood
                                      swim out to sea.

      that a decomposed emperor made threatening
       gestures.       Defiance!   --paid off the
                   government & smirked his
                              way to New Buenos Aires.

                      O fell in
                      the cement
                      cheated on
                      the rent
                      borrowed on
                      the grain &
                      fruit       &
                      pondered on the wave of
                        social unrest/      Spastic
            hopping legs         quick off to
                            the new world!

                        after the war
                    the population    of mixed ancestry
               Germans, Catholic Argentinians, Jiving Jews
                and Roman Japanese         embraced the
                        People's Republic of China

                  dealt in money excesses    & prevented
              sweet strife         & the spying        on
                        of     Uranus & Neptune

                                          ejaculated
                                          radio semen
                                          intensified
                                          the neutral
                                            metals
              & ruled with a
                            dictatorship &
                        laughed while fornicating & bull/
                          dozing on the Arctic ice
```

>in the fifties we all revered ole ez pound
>> & now we pay a buck 29 fr
>>> ground round!

>> & KNOW that ez pound
>> was derailed by FATHER TYME!

LII
Wild-Man & The Contemplation Of Lunar Incest

there's almost NO LIMIT
to thinking in terms of miscellaneous Blood Groupings

WILD-MAN!
WYLD-MAYN!
WILDE-MAHN!
WHILD-MANE!

                                               & so to radio-iodide
multi-movements & shortness
                       clear causes/ culture in
                      artificial energy fueling,   excess
          of grueling unknown streaming blood conditions

     V I V A   W I L D - M A N !

do the eyes look strange to you?   then check

           the mother
           is she Sicilian?
           Felonious intercourse/ sure quick vomit fast!

in case of rape
in case of incest
in case of
                black & blue veins
      do you smell
         strange aromas?   Lunar highlands
                           O neutral metals

             the planets are large & the surfaces
    furious   the forces of the thick atmosphere

           spring bigly   & cause minor
      night sweating   of animals & friendly
    injuns   Animal Bites!

                  romance of the rose
        the christian mystics the hydraulic
      press & reverence & gas engines & iron
    lungen   burning your Bunsen!
         fract/uring your calculating
       machine!
         So sweet.

LIII
Wild-Man & The Essence Of The Crystal X-Rays

         free
       with death the Power Project
will   c o n t i n u e
         rolling over &
      crashing s u b m e r g i n g
life in Andorra
quickening the
babe fast
into War wound
existence
       Voices on the Moon were heard
     on Earth the infusion of
     spice into the
     old easygoing
     exploited brown-skin
      race spice is nicer
  than boasting chinese
   Socialism/ sez FRANCE. more Power!
more Meat! more Spies! more military coups!
more Zealots!
       that they are beginning to make
      an effort following the
    clashes the overthrowing the
third dose
the time for body resistance to gory
peoples' protests. Selah!

         & Wild-Man & General
   stonewall jackson smelled out the sale
  of rum
 & the meeting of black slaves from Egypt & new raw
Bangkok   that the world faces
    the man who the police say is the purple thief
    the man who understands the problem
    the Wild-man who WILL
        slay the owners of
       rubber trees & tin mines
       & plastic corn stalks/
licentious Higher Education for the
Coatzacoalcos indians
       the middle-class movement
      into inspiration!
        the harmony in
       which a
      woman's position

                        is determined by
        her praise of
                                crystal X-rays!

LIV
Wild-Man & The Reverberation Of Poetry

```
                              & one is says,
                              I desire thee
               final & passing      the
vision
the thrust
                      becoming the dead cold
                                       & moving to what
                                I am/      &
                         knowing


                              the man sees Wild-Man crawl
            ing with         Suns
                                       created
                                    hung/slung Tung Bu
                pouring       the         moment     as trees drop
            old bark
                         & then with radiant
                                  energy
                                    &


                                                  reverberation
feeling
I KNOW.
We love.
                      but the soundless
                                                  the shining
                                                  rain
                          speaks dead heart



                 the pipes of TRANSLUCENCE!    steel/
                                               bunch
                                               before
                                               War
                                               kiss
                                               the
                                               violets.
                                               sing &
                                               enter
                                               that
                                               emanation
                                               muscle
                                               stumble
```

             light   the what is
       my song   red flower droop
 ing   sad.

.

LV
The Organization In The Jungle

      10,000 times   the
  circuit with largest bunch of violets
the 7.1% common fraction of life the forces produce
      white & purple
            influences
   of power To call

     the landscape grand flow

       the earth
        is farmland the
   ceremonial palaces croak Sexual Attraction

       the part
           the microwave tapers
     gravitation
        natural sections

     /Territory is scenic beauty so
   killing/ly rare

      the hope is the

      loose mad exile to begin
   to leave the wave of
      secrets
      which despite
      the spears
      rule the
      lowest in the world

   is noise cropping up
   the head of the sheep
   waves in jungle growth
   The area extends below 60 degrees S.

  the disputed islands in the South

         theocratic worms
     fill up in the hot & dry
   lunatik desert .the heaven

           drops glass
    & rust
                    Wild-Man chews a blade of grass.

LVI
The Mystery Of Wild-Woman & The Perfect Peace

                               floods   point   the
      westward migration   reproduce the
                                                extra
                                                energy

    reconvert it   to SOUTHWESTERN ASIA   AFRIKA

                          memory of the
               Attraction of a celestial body for
                               Zero

  physical change of   mantowoman   wild-woman
                         the catalyst of change/

                      GREAT!
                                    call the manifestation
   vision receiver   Rare-Earth

                                          it
                                          continues
                                          to
                                          end
                                          for
                                          him/
                                          wild-
                                          woman
                                          Saviour
                                          of
                                          Juice

        & the land is luxuriant   frag
                                          rant with
                                          voodoo
           excess of bloodshed
                                          rose in a
                                          prime womb/ a
                     trembling hydrogen bomb sweet
                       mucous & texturous
              Sacred design
                            throughout &
  swarming everywhere the sucking bees the food juice
  turning to her blood/her peace, perfect peace

                        Time
         cuts back
              to
           Her power.   flat rock.

LVII
Wild-Woman & The Nature Of Horror & Love

                    the glowing   the blue
broken   solid/earth   melting   I did
      BEHOLD   the field of Sloth
                                  & eye
              of GOD
        the mental
          soul cleansing
                the body/& with a SWORD
      purifying
            the Awakening

    the first is weight
      & white crying sky
  /the second is
  hanging tongue &
joined fingers   & yellow crookedness

        transform & Exalt!
        force the slipping
            S N A K E the beast
     taste of darkness &
       pure DIsTORtion

   how can you make the distinctions
/utter three sounds?

          this bird
          this wind
          this now/
          this pain
          this passion/
          this new-born
          two pieces of
          frog
this chunk of
stiff-necked barbaric
piss-pride!
          this wish for/
          virtue   when the song
   of wild-woman

      is the nature of horror
through Love

          .know me like the Sea.

O Beware!

LVIII
Wild-Woman & The Thinking-On Of Putrefaction

                                            the subsoil in
                     the territory
  &birds were found living   the binding power
                   was joyful

                                 now Woman has thrown
             the scientific cowardice   the
        mocking forbidden

                  street
                  sewer
                         the distant backdrop
   Divine service   the matter
                  of the
                  skin
                        the sun between the

                spine
                bones
                       wonder of unknown cause

generation of the nucleus/
                         the TOTAL MASS

                        to bombing &
                        construction
        an eagle flies over
  the   ravages   of Frozen waste   & disappears
to warm regions

                      the approach
                      to home &
                      the land
                      The wealth
                      of Great Rivers
                      the winging
                      System
                      readily
                      exploitable

        made into desert (interior)

                                vileness in industry
                                consumption in Pacific
                                Ocean   A hostile
                                climate   makes birds
sluggish

LIX
Wild-Woman And The Heart Of Things

                            the swollen   year
the single time   endless   falling down the night the
         awareness   of the death
                     of spreading leaves   the
                 purged   spiritinevil poured
    water   of horror

        what I did today   my mouth born
with such beauty   I describe the source of
fishkill light

        I Have Met The Spirit Before
      near mountain-high flames

  & have ye seen the god with the leather-ball
sitting in the jealous circle?
                     She was herself
                     dead   on earth
                     she smiled &
                     threw off her
                     shield/

    possessed by the
    last existence   the next
    phase   of the shimmering
    heart of things

                /As if all
                the old structures
                the decayed regions
                not even a foul speck
                on earth
captures the perpetual   springing world! Selah.

                we are
                very tenacious/
                the prey in the maw
                of the hyena
                inspired by the song/
                     of fury.

        I received from my father

    slow
    drizzle   great seriousness

I have made the fluid burn!

LX
Wild-Woman And The Device Of Mangling

                              leaving behind
                    the animals   breakdown of
         the beginning   the judgement of separation
                         until the death &
    sacrifice.   the

                    cuts of Rolled Iron and
                        Steel Products the
                        chemicals &
                        Power Machinery
                            metallurgy   the lunatik
                National Anthem   forces . anathema

                                slow sigh   .
                            hiss . slooc . soo .
                    gsp.

                            I fix my attention on
                A skeleton   reconciliation between particles &
        ME   I suggest the
                        value of
                        weakness   to go to bed
                                    without undressing
                                    and move the lever
                                    deal in cattle
                whisk   away   the
                        human form   I Am A Wonder Worker
                                I glance at others' eyes
                                I appear with wings and
                                a striking-fast switch
                            blade

                                    I smash
                obstructions
                            I cause acid to eat any
                    sort of hope
                                I dry up
                                    the wetness of plants
                            I hold a device
                            and . mangle
                        it is the day of . derision

102

LXI
Wild-Woman And The Vale Of Bones

                                    not in that great
      matter   contained   the extreme
                     Star   the depraved
            guides   transforming   this process

                     the view point does not
fear the taboo   all human
                  rose   made
                  positive once
                  again is a
                  turtle
                             the old loving
history   the spirit   what cannot be known?

                                   & by the power
    I lift   endlessly   I believe   the
                            Spring and Autumn
                            judgement
                         Since   the current
       forces
       forces   these words   it is a
return   .to the dirt.   extinction   no
                                           no
              not. to be.

      what shows?
      especially the beauty
        of the world   here &
now. The void.   the
              R
            E
               al Ity
                           directed
with the teachings
                          mother & daughter
                          of the earth

        between heaven
        you see the balanced
        order

                And rotten bones.

LXII
Wild-Woman & The Profound Wishing

                                      it is not what the
      present permanence   is   it perishes

                                    the condition
    is
craving.   from one
             the 3rd state
             I am rescued
                           I function profoundly.
         I am
         of gold   Wishing
                      Wishing
                           the kingly rule

     my   brilliance   is the state
                     of force become the Sun/
        the green purify/ed
                    &&
                        eternal

       drench &
       burn   laugh &
       find   gather &
       stroke strike down
       the evil nature/ O Empty!

                         this is what binds
  first   a thousand years   the
       comfort   new-born thus true
    existence
                    celebration of two wings
           of a bird
                        the body
      rising
             forming &
              wishing the
           presence
        & gazing wonder
                    the motion of
     the Answer
                is folding
                life back
                to blood.

LXIII
Wild-Woman In The Windless Night

                                                    tell   the
doom   white
              smile   forsaken

                   O a thing   lonely

            gizzard-grin

                                  head of a fractured
clown.   glaring   pale-green   eye   zzz

                  at the upper part
           of the jaw

                        drool   decay.

    with mad hands   they HANG on   a compound
of living
  death.   malice on the good name
            biting muscle-game
            elastic nether world
            come now, we must plan

                            the planting.

there is the fact of dancing in mid-air   flying
         thru   the   light   like
            a rubber ball

                       Because it's
  cool both halves   Scatter   the blast/

                beetles split to a
      Primary Cell
               in the windless
        night.

                    whatever
    is   protected   is unbroken   Not
within the cavity
    between things   the poem of silence.

LXIV
Breathing With Honey

              the Smile   involves   Pestilence

part of a fish   no joy.   nothing is born
            this   month   the mechanism

    puzzles   We Know   the instinkt

                    is a patch within
      memory

                   at the time of Milk
       moving quickly
       saturating the
       clusters of
       flowers   Peace is
the building material within a
                    generation   of
   fragrance.
           glowing white. Selah!

       I enkindle hum
          an
          ity   clearness sing.

A bursting & inhaling in the inward search

                          the breathing
    with honey

                  the first fruit of courage
  furious bubble   the moon between full Sun

                  the wishbone
       spirals toward the state of
      originating   the slime-worm
   is holy
               it moves from place to
  place   its like   is food   its   song
is wine   From mucus
            our Heads emerge

                  we lie face-up & laugh
    at the Atomic sun
                            sometimes
                    we say   fungus O fungus!

LXV
The Victim Sings Freshly

```
                                        yield!  & tell
        me counsel                 the form     of the right
                    Star                       it comes by
                            the wrathful    the hungry
                killer              who is fulfilled


                                the pleasure        light-quick
                striking the black rock      the hallowed
        earth          it's rolling        from inside
                    our mind     body     everlasting
                            is perception
                                           I practise
                breathing      it is my mouth       that is
        excellent          I believe this.

                                        walking in
                        kindness       what is good in me?
        the might of injected
                    steam        I throw the knife
                in boldness        the Victim sings
                        freshly & gushes
                    water from his side

                                    what is hooking?
                        where is    the deadly eye
                hiding        who conceals?

                                        a block on
        the crust     of the earth     is ready to flame
                matter sings to it!  Scolding earth!

                                what belongs to the
        weasel?     fleet
                    foot & crying tongue.

                                        a cause is
                    adventure      Salt formation
                            of a kiss

                                        terror Earth
                                        & good fat duck
                                        sniff geranium
                                        & give a fuck---


        afore          .we turn white.
```

LXVI
Wild-Woman & The Closeness Of The Gasp

```
                        IT IS THE WORDING      3
              justice/   it sweeps       the      Heaven        &
      earth       the land is forced
                              to eyesight (reality)
   Pure    true    the Mind    the   second   of    growing life.

                              I embrace  the
                                         conduct
                             the function
                            of original nature
                        the desire of looking on the
                   gold fluid the strength always exists
         it
         is
      for ever
                         where is the time of trapping
                      the effect of being
                      the lump     of
     death?      slow    it     is    in    china

  so far      away.
                                 I stir
                                 then in
                                 the mystery
                                 of the
                                 breath a
                                 belief a
                                 gasp a
                                 taste of
                                 the Name the
                                 long dazzling
                                 sound like
                                 plucking with
                                 the holy
                                 fingers
                                 I have had
                                 my day
                                 often &
                                 the inner
                                 light has
                                 been
                                 excessively
                                 Christly
                                 I think it
                                 has irrigated
```

                        the world.

    what a flood the 2nd time.   speak
                                        in the place of
                    shocking love

Part 4: Basic Information

LXVII
The Equinox Commandment

                              I glance with
           the   EYE   nothing is
          quiet   O no idleness   the parasite is
       laughing   we are anesthetized &
      free   of thrilling   what is brought to a
           level   of peace?
what is white derangement?   who carried the young
         backwards to travail?
                             the mother strips
              the corn-husk   she gives the child
       the bone of the world
                           with a steel nail
                     a comma is etched   it is
                     a pause on the child's
                    heart
                              except each other
              with abundant   ball-to-leg   grief
       we are cooking with
    love   the brown grain
                  numbers billions in our
                brain
                                 I am going eastward
                           for a meal with
                       out Anger   my spirit
                   is Untouched &
                   Breathing
                                     a green Parrot
         a thousand years long-living speaks
            my stage-
       directions.   I will not plunder
                      with a sword of
                      crazy steel

           my energy will
         spring   & disperse in my
       holy   self.
                              my compassion
                        is sun   gleaming &
                     eternal.
                     where is
                 the warmth.

LXVIII
Kaddish For The Father

                        the activity of   the whole
striking/   Pure Death   thrust   Father taken
                    Up   in his work
             The Time
          Of My
     Breath   the father's Power is
    another   a sharp break
           Sunlight & Moonlight   & Never
    dear O Sun lovely
    father we must go
    back to the source
    the hymn itself.
    enough left Time
    to teach you every/
    thing   do your Best!
do your Best!   numbers the
       double triple quadruple quintuple
    the supreme limited earth

                          father of Purity
                          Anger   I now bring
                          back   this Time
                          the cry of your
                          belief & legend

       you learned in your skin flesh bone/
unWorthy
                the way to heaven   is
            struggle against
              earth.   the rain in no time
     Again   cries   Out!
                        Ironically my dad
                        dy died from poison
                        ed blood that liquif
                        ied his liver/

       the one principle
         of pain   for the neck of a horse
           & my father

        tell me the force   of the strange
  wind?
             I ask what
             he thinks
             of this

LXIX
The Wandering / The Poem For The Father

```
                              this Night    Now
          is cold ,       cold ,    listen        your
minute        is      another    spasm
                                        you walk
                    drawing the darkness     around
       your breath                        bringing
                         eye-lid        down
                                        fast.

            you    have    no
                           gusto
                anymore

                          I perform
                          Song
                          into
                          the
                          veins
                          of
                          your
    rot/    soul history offering of        .mud
                                                thus
                      dead       you    are
                      happy   &         Earth is
                bloody-yellow

                      You surprised me
                      when you died

             I wanted to sit
          with you            in a circle
                  saying magic
     words.
                           there is
                           a new name
                           for rain
                           today.
                           the poetic
                           transformation
                           of feet &
                           hands
                           the very light
                           song of father
                           into
```

the
earth.

LXX
The Father Song — A Continuation

                                                the milk pail   whose?
          the   blue   eye   whose?   the
cow's is
   purple-orange   the tit   the tooth   the claw
                       the roaming

               byrning tyger
                                      what oozes?
    whose search?
                        the father of ourself
            the principle   of
      grief
           there is a city I have not
visited   its rule
       is called Mystery!
                                Pop-Eye
   the fryer   of   small-fish

        says:
              Contend With Thy Father!

that I might not have
(of the year)
been weak or strong
that I might have
perished &
been stretched out--

                even a beggar buying &
           selling comic books   playing a
        violin under the BMT

    My mental Nature dislikes
      putting   a finger   on death

I wouldn't stoop so low   to feel dissatisfaction with
                the calm   monster
                                 He
               of systematized
                  fear-less-ness   the
      stinging
              cutting down
                        the removal
   of   light

LXXI
The Father Weeping — & The Machine

```
                              M
                              A
                              G
                              I
                              C        O  I
        am weary      of not         doing anything
  I have stated    IT
                         Nothing O Zero
                                          the exterior
       change       I learn to think
                  with an insistent       emotion.

  Was a free woman free?    higher
                            knowing than

                            the nerves
                            of gold?

                            the question
                            the nerves

                            of earth-black      black
                wound
             & Song!

                              No doubt
                              as the wild-man
                              the free-man
                              the fallen away
                wound
           Star!
                                    Our nerves achieve
                               the deepened
                   living                      the nerves
                                               repeat
                                            are changed
                                       to        the nerves

                He found out    Father Why Hast Thou
      let the nerves    dissolve!
                                        I thought.
```

118

                         my peaceful
              new
         beliefs   naught go
                    to the
grave.

LXXII
The Father Joy — The Running

                        the Sun   And deadly
    cluster   the heart of the
        marshes
              how can you explain that
I move thru electricity
          yields which see
          picker tool azzaz

          the most meaningful
          event of my life

          is my death.

                    I would not be
    turned to   Coal   for the world.
                            into
  breath.   maybe.

                and daffodils & marvelous
        mong-dung.
            I'd like to ask you in
closing   for the basic   kind of positive
                          local
       mobilization of
       people   O bring all people
           together!

                        I have fed this
   emotion   into the sand
       of my
   proportion   what Am I ?

       onion, Rock
       Maple,
       my Human existence

                       that I called
   the twenty seconds   I stepped on Quiet Feet

  All Praises   to the Ground   we are guided

        to the relief

of colour　　we speckle the
　　　　　　egg.
　　　　　　the harbour
　　　　　　the text
　　　　　　the sound
of day

LXXIII
The Young Father — But That Was In Another Country

                                         Speak   within the
Shout!   the following   vain internal culture
                                                                    uniting
                         all liberation   Beings
Bong!
                never draw
                a hundred
                silences   the Morning is
finished   yes,
                eagles
                eyes
                sap the
                energy
                in the cave.

                Kindle the duality
                each exchange of
                ice   gives us
                Hope!
                                    if I could have frozen
                        myself I would have eaten
                        apple-tart with you/

          sit on my grave   Jerusalem
          mutters on the
      radio.   a-sailing we will
              go
                sleepy-head
                                blood is
                          clearish   mud.
          I flash smiles at
G-d   all the day

                    begin with
                    a boy's beginning
                    loving in
                    Vienna   I
        laughed when my parents died   but falsely
                because I was   so afraid
       of the
    Germans   I made believe I was jewish-invisible

                    in Austria we didn't   know
     the
                Baal-Shem
                                   .selah.
          forgive.

LXXIV
The Spoken Father Word

                        and places hills   Shut the
World   reach   the water lily

                                       the minute of
              the middle   of that century
       the looking
       into the point of
                    f o r m

                             the mucus/
                         regulation of
                            The judgement of
        Morning
            the gleam
            of a scientist
            spoiling the
            Now
                    the zealousness
        of bone-crushings &
      The Second Coming
      of enemies

                   O Woe O Woop O Hum
crackpot!   What is the master of   the inch of
                  first crime?

                         Sorrow,
                         noises,
                         conscious beings
      spinning in the offensive   the dash
to thought   and earth   Draw your eyes
                    back to yr
                    spine

        practice reasoning   the bleeding

      the distribution
                        of perfect dreams
                 So the feet suck the rain &
     point   to the End
                     the desirable
          stage   of small
      energy.

LXXV
The Father Whispering Away In The Earth

                    I Will See the Sources
   the fluid   the meat that sleeps
                         the neighbor's
                         eye   the just
                         stopped heart
                         the fool's
gleam   of nothing at all!
                      our children are still
      eating up the heaven

                           there is
         nothing for me to roll
    toward   I was the first to leave
the sticking side   of beef   the corpse
      that still sweats

    that says 'hello'   Now begin to
               grimace
         Know your lips
        Know your nine
    sounds   of first the worm
     & then the water
     & then the   hole.

  & how it feels   to need   the Sun's
Milk
      what was done?
      who jumped?
      say what is
      making music?
      way down what
      talks? down where
      does who walk?
      extend your leg
      & jump   to the dogs?
      Imitate the dream
      of my   laugh
      fool around with
      my death   & pray
      the powerful   gristle
      away.

you wonder what's in the ground
a small brown nut
a fragment of broken tractor
rusted   laying next to a bit
of hobo-comb

LXXVI
The Father Whispering All The While

                                        I tell you so   did it
    have the loneness?
                 this world between
                 my lips
                       the dust
                       the failure
                       of the pit
                       reflecting
                       to the point
                       of the cosmic
                       revealing/   light the
                                       confusion
   the foot sticketh in the mud
                       I Am a flower

          goat

        sparrow

      weed radiating in the dusk

           the gift to being

       ye/S!   this order

                         once when i was young i
       walked to the park   i sat on a wood bench
     i saw the order of the galaxy   the river
    of angels   the wandering down to eat
   some crystal flakes   the movement
of giant   old   old   root

                   a woman
                   everywhere
                   beyond
                   the bird
                   shaking
                   lying
                   everywhere
                   stopping
                   fishing
                   the vision
                   out of
                   the curve
                   of contradiction

oak face! O old
nickel for a
pickle!

LXXVII
The Father Destiny — Love

                                                                             & advancing to the
      Departure   who drops dead   especially without a
smile. a high voice   breaking the goodness
                                                  of a lung

                  they laugh & dance
          out of the supreme Wish!
      everything everything   with sounds!
                            so now stretch
                            the number one
                            my dying my
                            bending whole-
                            ness sinking
                            under the rain
                            the slope of
                            my power drop-
                            ing

           when i
           am cold

           i rep-
           eat

           when i
           shoot

           & fert-
           ilize

           the gro-
           und

           so i give
           you the

           search of
           my self

           the end
           of my

           quiet.
           that way
                                      over there.

LXXVIII
The Father Wounding Into Star

       looking at me High
   & catching the weakened night time the
 white   entered sun/light coming & fighting
 the blossom that cries
       sneerup! the worm
       digs its little
       lips into my
  thi/gh. O I didn't think
I would see   what happens
    when we die.

      do you think
      that my gums
      throb good-bye. Yes!

      what food
      is the noise
      in the ground.

    i go away
    smiling & disappearing
    with loose teeth

   before you guess
   what rots under
   the grass praise me!
        that i once was
        dancing vigorously

     & smoothing my
     hands one on the other
     all mine! all mine!

  i have fulfilled the living song/
   round my
  body folds
 & seeps into
the breath of
  day
      white gulp
      of driving end
      i sense a TREE
      FLOWERING
        above me.

LXXIX
The Father's Looking-On & Proof

        My value is growing
  into Speech of the moon. & bowing
  my face   & showering & breaking the rays of my mouth.

        what is ripe? my wife lives/
 her gaze   has sparks.
      bursting
      forth
      into
      white
      senses
         sometimes the sun
       needs a word
     different from all the world
    the eye the brow the smiling
 feet.
           where
           emotion
           is a
           Lion's
           paw
           by layers
           the bones
           are grown
           blackening
           for truth
           the eight
           tips of
           branches
           my Fate
           is the
           Trees
           I suppose
           my beak
           was always
           poor.

   well blessing   the beauty
       of the hole to freedom
     I swallow
   the icy
  wind.
      i'm heading onward.

LXXX
Father's Expression Into Air

                                          towards the Atomic century
the Alphabet   driven into fire   two demons
            keeping commandment
      a motorized fiend
   concluding the
moment

                   a pig's dialogue/

          1,2,3,   touching the concrete
     the next knife closing the
   mystery of wondering &
poetry
                 both devils are happy.

       or
       before
       the
       proof
       the
       genuine
       wish
       a
       superb
       natural
       task
       the
       death
       in
       two
       different
       stories
       a primitive
       Name
       Elohim
       the
       expression
       of a
       language
       into
       Air

showing
the
joke
of my
laugh &
HYMN

LXXXI
The Question Of Father Exalting

                        ruthless White Radishes
                      RubAdub   what took place
          please, die?   a question
not crying   in   CrakoW   Hawk-Toothed
                  land-Owners Yow!

              I recognize
         the transcended   self-of not   Death!

              the present
              frightening
             image of
            force-feeding
        geese   Here we had the Scriptures
to slumber next to   a bed of Hard Stone to
              surround our flesh

       the sod is hod in Crakow YOW!

                I was never merry with Singing
          I rearranged the rare time of my
       floating blood
    I kissed the
quick smile
   of the valiant
Suffering Sun/
                     my stolen Weeds
              drowned & turned to nothing/

        we sold 3 Radishes White as White Teeth
      in Vietnam   the asians come even in
              our rivers,
         the light voices
           in the pocket
      of earth
                      scream: Evil!
               RubaDub
             slime/
             rhyme/
        YI-YAW-YOW!
Dost Thou Mock My veins.
                no question.

LXXXII
The Father Of Quest — Swallowing The Silence

                                        the thing in the Head
      the Apple   the planet of ripe bull-
Shit   what it transforms   what it uses what
it bids us do   sometimes we are fixed back
        wards   toward the week
   of White laughter

                       the skin
                       is using the
                       Verse it shines
                       Axle grease
                       it swears by the
                       Hand of the
                       Creator   with vulgarity
        & deception   with a void of
     grimaces   with the mutter of trembling
            Atmosphere
                       wine swelling the
                       grey breast of death
                       the breathing burnt
                       the end
         of   quest.   Swallows   Silences
  the learning
  mud sickling the body
                    from the Weight of
        madness

                            O how when the born
               god of love fries   squats
           on An
   Egg   seeks the ant   to fulfill & draw near
silky clouds shaking
When the hill is full-jumping of Love
                       dull-ness
                       make-shift
                       charge & lunge
                       crank the Heart
                       beat the wet-ness
                       the Shaky
                       Knowledge
                       falling under the bed
                       of dust
                       single-strand

of pity
poor-piece
body full of worms

Printed October 1974 in Santa Barbara &
Ann Arbor for the Black Sparrow Press by
Noel Young & Edwards Brothers Inc. Design
by Barbara Martin. This edition is published
in paper wrappers; there are 200 hardcover
copies numbered and signed by the author;
& 26 copies handbound in boards by Earle
Gray lettered & signed by the author.

Rochelle Owens is the award-winning author of many controversial and innovative plays, and a pioneer in the experimental Off-Broadway movement. Her plays have been performed throughout the world and presented at festivals in Paris, Berlin, Edinburgh and Rome. She has published four books of poetry, the most recent being part of the series **The Joe Chronicles**, two collections of plays, **Futz And What Came After**, and **The Karl Marx Play And Others**. She has edited **Spontaneous Combustion: Eight New American Plays**. Her poetry and plays appear in many journals and anthologies. She has given numerous poetry readings as well as recording her adaptations of primitive and archaic world poetry. She is on the board of directors of the Women's Interart Center. She is a Guggenheim Fellow and has spent a year at the Yale School of Drama as an ABC Fellow in Film Writing. She lives with her husband, the poet George Economou, in New York City, and recently completed a long choral work, **The Joe Oratorio.**